D1611356

Desert
HABITATS

BY ARNOLD RINGSTAD

Published by The Child's World®
1980 Lookout Drive • Mankato, MN 56003-1705
800-599-READ • www.childsworld.com

Acknowledgments
The Child's World®: Mary Berendes, Publishing Director
Red Line Editorial: Editorial direction
The Design Lab: Design
Amnet: Production

Photographs ©: Oleg Znamenskiy/Shutterstock Images,
cover, 1; Eric Isselee/Shutterstock Images, back
cover, 22; Shutterstock Images, back cover, 6–7, 14;
Brand X Pictures, 5; Chris Howey/Shutterstock Images, 8;
Bill Perry/Shutterstock Images, 10–11; Mike Norton/
Shutterstock Images, 13; Hagit Berkovich/Shutterstock
Images, 17; Alersandr Hunta/Shutterstock Images, 18;
Tim Roberts Photography/Shutterstock Images, 21

ISBN 9781623239893
LCCN 2013947267

Printed in the United States of America
Mankato, MN
December, 2013
PA02192

Table of Contents

Welcome to the Desert!

Deserts are all over Earth. They are on every continent. Many people think deserts are hot, sandy places where nothing can survive. But deserts can be hot or cold. And they are full of life. Plants and animals live on the ground. Birds fly in the sky.

Only rain forest habitats have a larger variety of plants and animals than deserts.

It is not easy to live in deserts. Plants and animals have **adapted** to live there. Some desert animals do not even need to drink water! Living things work together to survive. Desert plants create shade. This guards animals from the hot sun.

The world's deserts are in danger. **Climate** change is making deserts hotter and drier. Human activities can poison and ruin the landscape. These activities put plants and animals in danger.

Desert habitats can be hard places to live. Animals and plants adapt to life here.

Where Are the World's Deserts?

All seven continents have deserts. The biggest non-polar desert is the Sahara. It is in North Africa. The Sahara is almost as big as the United States. The Arabian Desert and the Gobi Desert are other large deserts. The Arabian Desert is in the Middle East. The Gobi Desert is in Asia.

There are many other deserts. The United States has the Mojave Desert. Australia has many deserts. This area is also called the Outback. The Atacama Desert in South America is the driest place in the world. Mountains block water from reaching it. Some years the Atacama Desert gets no rain.

Deserts are found across the world on every continent.

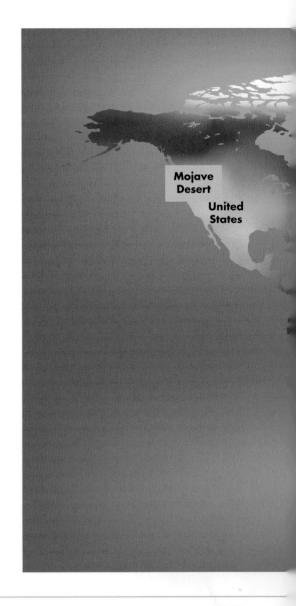

Mojave Desert

United States

Some people also call Antarctica a desert. This is the largest desert in the world. Very little **precipitation** falls here. Most of the water is ice. There is not much life in Antarctica.

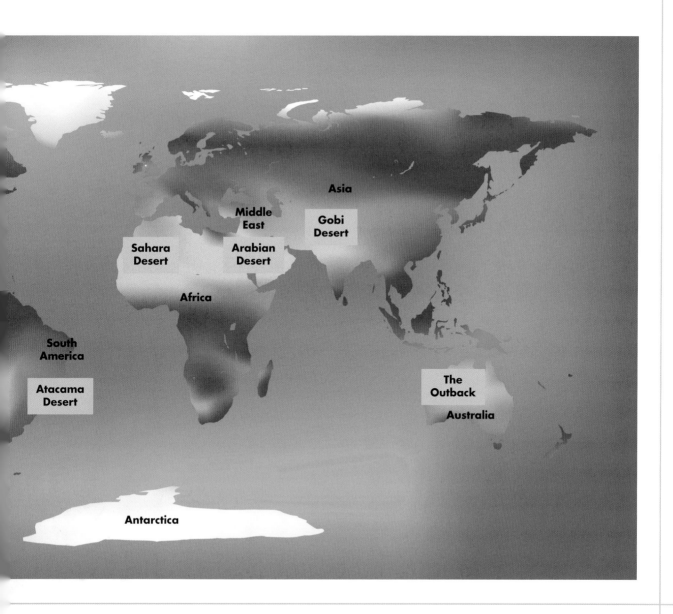

What Do Deserts Look Like?

There are three kinds of deserts. They are hot and dry, cool coastal, and semi-arid. Each kind has a different temperature range. They also have different soil, plants, and animals.

Hot and dry deserts are the hottest deserts. Some people think these deserts are full of sand. Only 10 percent of the world's deserts are sandy. Hot and dry deserts have rocky, shallow soil. Very little water is under the surface. The Sahara Desert is hot and dry.

Cool coastal deserts are found near oceans. The Atacama Desert in Chile is near the ocean. The ocean currents give these deserts lower temperatures. The soil usually has some salt in it. This is because of the nearby salt water.

Semi-arid deserts have soil that is either bumpy or smooth. Parts of the United States have semi-arid deserts. They look similar to hot and dry deserts. But semi-arid deserts do not get as hot. They also do not get as cold at night. There is usually no water under the soil.

The edge of the Atacama Desert in Chile is near the Pacific Ocean.

The Driest Places on Earth

Not all deserts are hot. But all deserts are dry. Deserts get less than 10 inches (25 cm) of precipitation per year. Some deserts get much less than that.

Hot and dry deserts have very high temperatures. The Sahara Desert is the largest hot and dry desert. It can hit 122 degrees Fahrenheit (50°C). The hottest temperature on Earth is in a desert. In Death Valley in the Mojave Desert, the temperature once reached 134 degrees Fahrenheit (57°C).

Other deserts can become very cold. The Gobi Desert is one example of this. The temperature drops to −40 degrees

Death Valley in California is one of the hottest places on Earth.

Fahrenheit (−40°C) in the winter. The Gobi Desert does not get as hot as the Sahara Desert in the summer.

The word Gobi means "waterless place" in Mongolian.

The Plants of the Desert

One famous desert plant is the saguaro cactus. It is one of the world's largest kinds of cactus. Saguaros can grow 70 feet (21 m) tall. They grow in the United States and Mexico. They are very useful for desert animals. Their wide roots gather water from the soil. Birds peck holes in cacti and live inside. The cacti also make fruit that people and animals can eat.

The tallest Joshua tree in California is more than 40 feet (12 m) tall.

Another desert plant is the saxaul. This small tree grows in the Gobi Desert. Camels use the saxaul for food and shade. People who live in the Gobi Desert can get water from the tree. They take off the bark and press it to get water out.

The Joshua tree grows in the United States. It is not really a tree. It is a kind of plant called a yucca. This amazing plant can live for hundreds of years. It is used as food and housing by animals. Native Americans use the Joshua tree to make baskets.

Many saguaro cacti grow in the deserts of the southwestern United States and Mexico.

Beating the Heat

Not all deserts are hot. But the ones that are hot can be hard places to live. Many desert animals have ways to beat the heat.

Jackrabbits are **nocturnal**. They rest in the shade under bushes during the day. But they also have another way to keep cool. Their huge ears **radiate** heat away from their bodies.

Turkey vultures have another way to live in the heat. Scientists discovered their bald heads radiate heat. The wind cools their heads when they fly. This cools down the entire bird.

Lizards called Gila monsters stay out of the sun. They spend almost all their time in holes. They only leave to get food or warm up when it is cold. They can store fat in their tails. This means they do not need to eat often. Gila monsters can survive months without food.

Jackrabbits' huge ears help them stay cool in the desert.

Going without Water

Water is very important for life. But all deserts are very dry. So how do desert animals live in these places? They have adaptations and **behaviors** that help them survive.

Fennecs are tiny foxes that live in the Sahara Desert. They can go a long time without drinking. Most of their water comes from eating fruits and leaves. Their **kidneys** are specially adapted for the desert. They can store water for long periods of time. This keeps the fennecs from losing the water in their bodies.

Kangaroo rats live in North America. They got their name because they hop like kangaroos. They are not related to real kangaroos. Kangaroo rats can survive without water. Their bodies turn the dry seeds they eat into water. Also, it is **humid** in their underground holes. They take in water from the air they breathe.

Fennec foxes do not need a lot of water to survive.

The Amazing Bactrian Camel

The Bactrian camel lives in the Gobi Desert. This huge desert is in Mongolia and China. The Gobi is very cold and has little plant life. The Bactrian camel survives by being able to eat many different kinds of plants.

The camel can survive during long periods without food. The humps on its back help it survive. These camels have two humps. Many people think they store water in these humps. However, they actually hold fat. The camels use this fat to get energy. It lets them survive without food for many days.

Bactrian camels can also go a long time without drinking. They drink what they need when they find water. If they are not thirsty they drink a little. But if they are very thirsty they drink a lot. A thirsty camel can drink up to 30 gallons (114 L) in 10 minutes.

The Bactrian camel has adapted to life in the cold Gobi Desert.

Threats to the Desert

Desert plants and animals are great at surviving heat and dryness. But they are in danger from human activities that cause pollution and damage their habitat. These activities make deserts unsafe for plants and animals.

Too many people living near the desert also affects plants and animals. Farmers let their animals eat the plants on the edge of the desert. This leaves less for animals to eat.

Another big problem is climate change. It may make temperatures go up. It can also make it rain less. The little bit of water in the desert can dry up. Many desert plants and animals can survive with little water. But they cannot survive without any water at all.

Mining in the desert can also be harmful. People use chemicals to get gold out of the ground. These chemicals are poisonous to plants and animals. The cars and trucks people use are also a danger. Driving across the desert can harm plants and animals even more. Taking care of the world's deserts helps them continue to survive.

Desert mines are dangerous for the plants and animals that live here.

GLOSSARY

adapted (uh-DAPT-ed) Adapted is adjusting to conditions. Animals and plants have adapted to life in the desert.

behaviors (bi-HAYV-yuhrs) The way animals act are behaviors. Desert animals have learned behaviors that help them survive.

climate (KLYE-mit) Climate is the weather over a long period of time. Climate change is making deserts hotter and drier.

humid (HYOO-mid) Having a lot of water in the air means it is humid. Kangaroo rats live in humid homes.

kidneys (KID-nee) Kidneys control the body's water. Fennec foxes have specially adapted kidneys.

mining (MINE-ing) Mining is digging for minerals in the earth. Mining in the desert is harmful.

nocturnal (nok-TUR-nuhl) Being active at night is nocturnal. Jackrabbits are nocturnal.

precipitation (pri-sip-i-TAY-shuhn) Rain or snow is precipitation. There is very little precipitation in the desert.

radiate (RAY-dee-ate) Radiate means to remove heat from. Some desert animals radiate heat.

TO LEARN MORE

BOOKS

Bennett, Paul. *Desert Habitats (Exploring Habitats)*. Milwaukee, WI: Gareth Stevens, 2007.

Kalman, Bobbie. *A Desert Habitat*. New York: Crabtree, 2007.

Sill, Cathryn. *About Habitats: Deserts*. Atlanta, GA: Peachtree, 2012.

WEB SITES

Visit our Web site for links about desert habitats:
childsworld.com/links

Note to Parents, Teachers, and Librarians: We routinely verify our Web links to make sure they are safe and active sites. So encourage your readers to check them out!

INDEX

ABOUT THE AUTHOR

Arnold Ringstad lives in Minnesota. He likes to visit the local zoo so he can see animals from all kinds of habitats.